The NFL's Greatest Teams

ATLANTA FALCONS

Big Buddy Books

An Imprint of Abdo Publishing
abdopublishing.com

Katie Lajiness

abdopublishing.com

Published by Abdo Publishing, a division of ABDO, PO Box 398166, Minneapolis, Minnesota 55439.
Copyright © 2017 by Abdo Consulting Group, Inc. International copyrights reserved in all countries. No part
of this book may be reproduced in any form without written permission from the publisher. Big Buddy Books™
is a trademark and logo of Abdo Publishing.

Printed in the United States of America, North Mankato, Minnesota.
092016
012017

THIS BOOK CONTAINS
RECYCLED MATERIALS

Cover Photo: ASSOCIATED PRESS.
Interior Photos: ASSOCIATED PRESS (pp. 5, 7, 9, 11, 13, 14, 15, 17, 18, 19, 20, 21, 23, 25, 27, 28, 29);
    Kevin Terrell (p. 11).

Coordinating Series Editor: Tamara L. Britton
Graphic Design: Michelle Labatt, Taylor Higgins, Jenny Christensen

Publisher's Cataloging-in-Publication Data

Names: Lajiness, Katie, author.
Title: Atlanta Falcons / by Katie Lajiness.
Description: Minneapolis, MN : Abdo Publishing, 2017. | Series: NFL's greatest
    teams | Includes bibliographical references and index.
Identifiers: LCCN 2016944890 | ISBN 9781680785272 (lib. bdg.) |
    ISBN 9781680798876 (ebook)
Subjects: LCSH: Atlanta Falcons (Football team)--History--Juvenile literature.
Classification: DDC 796.332--dc23
LC record available at http://lccn.loc.gov/2016944890

Contents

A Winning Team

The Atlanta Falcons are a football team from Atlanta, Georgia. They have played in the National Football League (NFL) for more than 50 years.

The Falcons have had good seasons and bad. But time and again, they've proven themselves. Let's see what makes the Falcons one of the NFL's greatest teams.

Black, red, silver, and white are the team's colors.

League Play

The NFL got its start in 1920. Its teams have changed over the years. Today, there are 32 teams. They make up two conferences and eight divisions.

The Falcons play in the South Division of the National Football Conference (NFC). This division also includes the Carolina Panthers, the New Orleans Saints, and the Tampa Bay Buccaneers.

The New Orleans Saints are a major rival of the Falcons.

Team Standings

The NFC and the American Football Conference (AFC) make up the NFL. Each conference has a north, south, east, and west division.

Kicking Off

The Atlanta Falcons became the fifteenth team to join the NFL. The Falcons were founded in 1965 by Rankin M. Smith Sr. The team began play in 1966. Like many new teams, the Falcons struggled. They didn't have a winning season until 1973.

Linebacker Tommy Nobis (60) played with the Falcons for ten years. In 2004, he joined the team's Ring of Honor.

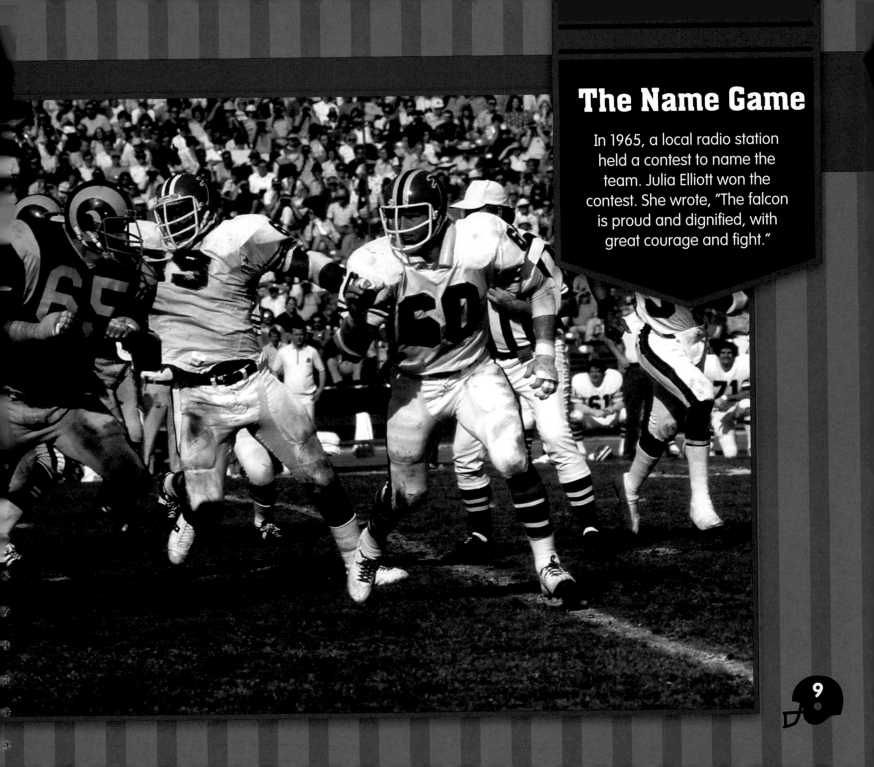

The Name Game

In 1965, a local radio station held a contest to name the team. Julia Elliott won the contest. She wrote, "The falcon is proud and dignified, with great courage and fight."

Highlight Reel

The Falcons have had many highs and lows. They made the play-offs in 1978, 1980, and 1982. But, from 1983 to 1990, the team finished every season with a losing record.

In 1998, the Falcons had their best season! They won their division with a team record of 14 wins. In the play-offs, the Falcons beat the San Francisco 49ers and the Minnesota Vikings. Then they played in their first Super Bowl. Sadly, the Falcons lost to the Denver Broncos 34–19.

The Falcons line up to play the Broncos in the 1999 Super Bowl.

In 1989, Deion Sanders made a 68-yard run for a touchdown! This was his first game with the Falcons.

The Falcons had an eight-game winning streak during the 2002 season. The team made it to the play-offs. They beat the Green Bay Packers 27–7. But they lost the next game to the Philadelphia Eagles 20–6.

In 2008, **rookie** quarterback Matt Ryan was the team's star player. He helped the Falcons reach the play-offs several times. The Falcons played in the NFC **championship** in 2013. But, they lost to the San Francisco 49ers.

In 2003, the Falcons made NFL history! They beat the Green Bay Packers in a play-off game at Lambeau Field.

Win or Go Home

NFL teams play 16 regular season games each year. The teams with the best records are part of the play-off games. Play-off winners move on to the conference championships. Then, conference winners face off in the Super Bowl!

The Falcons picked quarterback Matt Ryan (*right*) in the 2008 draft.

Halftime! Stat Break

Team Records

RUSHING YARDS
Career: Gerald Riggs, 6,631 yards (1982–1988)
Single Season: Jamal Anderson, 1,846 yards (1998)
PASSING YARDS
Career: Matt Ryan, 32,757 yards (2008–2015)
Single Season: Matt Ryan, 4,719 yards (2012)
RECEPTIONS
Career: "Roddy" White, 808 receptions (2005–2015)
Single Season: Julio Jones, 136 receptions (2015)
ALL-TIME LEADING SCORER
Morten Andersen, 806 points (1995–2007)

Famous Coaches

Leeman Bennett (1977–1982)
Dan Reeves (1997–2003)
Mike Smith (2008–2014)

Championships

SUPER BOWL APPEARANCES:
1999

SUPER BOWL WINS:
None

Pro Football Hall of Famers & Their Years with the Falcons

Claude Humphrey, Defensive End (1968–1978)
Deion Sanders, Cornerback/Kick Returner/Punt Returner (1989–1993)

Fan Fun

STADIUM: Mercedes-Benz Stadium
LOCATION: Atlanta, Georgia
MASCOT: Freddie Falcon

Coaches' Corner

In 1977, Leeman Bennett took over a struggling Falcons team. Bennett's defense allowed only 129 points in 14 games that season. It was an NFL record at the time. In 1978, the team went to the play-offs for the first time. And, they finally won their division in 1980.

Mike Smith became head coach in 2008. That season, the Falcons won 11 games and made it to the play-offs. He was named NFL Coach of the Year. Smith led the team to the play-offs again in 2010, 2011, and 2012.

Bennett was the first Falcons coach to have a career-winning record.

Smith coached the Falcons for seven seasons.

17

Star Players

Tommy Nobis LINEBACKER (1966–1976)

Tommy Nobis was the team's first pick in the 1966 **draft**. As a **rookie**, he set a team record with 294 tackles. That year, Nobis was named NFL Rookie of the Year. He was picked to play in five Pro Bowls, which is the NFL's all-star game.

Claude Humphrey DEFENSIVE END (1968–1978)

Claude Humphrey was a first-round pick in the 1968 **draft**. He won the NFL Defensive **Rookie** of the Year **award**. In 1977, he was a part of the Falcons record-setting defense. In 2014, Humphrey joined the Pro Football Hall of Fame.

Jeff Van Note CENTER (1969–1986)

Jeff Van Note was a star player who went to six Pro Bowls. He played with the team for 18 seasons. That is a Falcons record! In 1986, Van Note **retired** from the NFL.

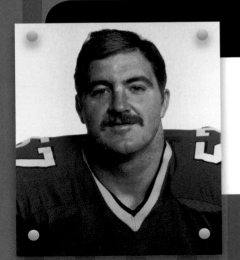

Steve Bartkowski QUARTERBACK (1975–1985)

Steve Bartkowski was the first pick in the 1975 **draft**. He was named NFL **Rookie** of the Year after throwing for 1,662 yards. Bartkowski set every team passing record, including 154 touchdown passes in 123 games.

Gerald Riggs RUNNING BACK (1982–1988)

Gerald Riggs was with the Falcons for seven seasons. He played in three Pro Bowls. In 1985, Riggs had his best year with the Falcons. He rushed for 1,719 yards and ten touchdowns.

Deion Sanders CORNERBACK/KICK RETURNER/ PUNT RETURNER (1989–1993)

Deion Sanders was a star athlete who played **professional** football and baseball. His big personality and athletic skills earned him the nickname Prime Time. During his time with the Falcons, he had ten touchdowns! Sanders became a member of the Pro Football Hall of Fame in 2011.

Matt Ryan QUARTERBACK (2008–)

In his first year with the Falcons, Matt Ryan threw for 3,440 yards. That was a team record for a **rookie** quarterback. Ryan won the NFL Offensive Rookie of the Year **award**. From 2008 to 2015, he passed for 32,757 yards. This set another team record!

Falcons Stadium

The Falcons play home games at the Georgia Dome. This stadium is in Atlanta. It opened in 1992.

In 2014, building began on a new stadium for the Falcons. Mercedes-Benz Stadium will be in Atlanta. It will hold up to 75,000 people.

Mercedes-Benz Stadium is expected to open in 2017.

The Georgia Dome was host to the 1994 Super Bowl. That year, the Dallas Cowboys beat the Buffalo Bills 30–13.

Rise Up!

Thousands of fans flock to home games to cheer on the Falcons. Some fans gather and walk from Centennial Olympic Park to the stadium. This is called the Falcon March.

The team's **mascot** is Freddie Falcon. He leads fans in a team **chant**! Fans yell, "Go, Falcons go!" when the team kicks the football off the tee.

Fans love to pose for pictures with Freddie Falcon!

Falcon fans wave red flags that read "Rise Up."

Falcons players used to perform a dance when they scored a touchdown. They called this dance the Dirty Bird.

Final Call

The Falcons have a long, rich history. They played in the 1999 Super Bowl. And, they will play in a brand new stadium in 2017.

Even during losing seasons, true fans have stuck by them. Many believe the Atlanta Falcons will remain one of the greatest teams in the NFL.

The Falcons beat the Seattle Seahawks at the 2013 NFC Divisional play-offs.

Through the Years

1966

The team plays its first game on September 11. They lose to the Los Angeles Rams 19–14.

1977

The team's defense is known as the Gritz Blitz. They allow the fewest points in NFL history.

1978

The Falcons make the play-offs for the first time.

1998

The Falcons have a 14–2 winning season. This is the best record in the team's history.

2002

Businessman Arthur Blank purchases the team from the Smith family.

2008

Coach Mike Smith and quarterback Matt Ryan join the Falcons. They lead the Falcons to the play-offs.

2014

Construction begins on the Falcons' new stadium. The stadium will open in 2017.

2012

The Falcons win their fifth division **championship**.

2015

Coach Dan Quinn becomes the team's 16th head coach.

29

Postgame Recap

1. What was the team's powerful defense in 1977 called?

   A. The Gritz Blitz   **B**. The Steel Curtain   **C**. The Dirty Birds

2. What year did the Falcons appear in the Super Bowl?

   A. 1997
   B. 1998
   C. 1999

3. Name the 2 Falcons players in the Pro Football Hall of Fame.

4. Which of these teams is a rival of the falcons?

   A. New Orleans Saints
   B. New England Patriots
   C. Denver Broncos

Glossary

award something that is given in recognition of good work or a good act.

championship a game, a match, or a race held to find a first-place winner.

chant a word or a phrase that is repeated to a beat. Usually, chants are spoken loudly by a crowd.

draft a system for professional sports teams to choose new players. When a team drafts a player, they choose that player for their team.

mascot something to bring good luck and help cheer on a team.

professional (pruh-FEHSH-nuhl) paid to do a sport or activity.

retire to give up one's job.

rookie a first-year player in a professional sport.

Websites

To learn more about the NFL's Greatest Teams, visit **booklinks.abdopublishing.com**. These links are routinely monitored and updated to provide the most current information available.

Index